Trope Trafficking

FIGURES OF SPEECH FOR CLASSICAL COMPOSITION

Student's Edition

EILEEN CUNNINGHAM

Edited by Amy Alexander Carmichael

Lochinvar Press

Table of Contents

Introduction

Aristotle reported in his *Poetics* how the comic playwright Ariphrades "ridiculed the tragedians for using phrases which no one would employ in ordinary speech" (e.g., writing *Achilleos peri,* "Achilles about," instead of *peri Achilleos,* "about Achilles"). But Aristotle set him aright by pointing out, "It is precisely because such phrases are not part of the current idiom that they give distinction to the style."[1]

Indeed, what sets literature apart from ordinary discourse is, in fact, this unusual use of words, which we call the *poetic quality* or the *artistic use* of the language. As Aristotle explained, in the best literature, "Every word is either current, or strange, or metaphorical, or ornamental, or newly-coined, or lengthened, or contracted, or altered."[2] Look at this example from Macbeth by William Shakespeare, where Lady Macbeth has just learned that King Duncan, whom she plans to murder, will stay at Macbeth's castle that night and leave "tomorrow":

1 O, never
2 Shall sun that morrow see!
3 Your face, my thane, is as a book where men
4 May read strange matters. To beguile the time,
5 Look like the time; bear welcome in your eye,
6 Your hand, your tongue: look like the innocent flower,
7 But be the serpent under't.[3]

Lines 1-2 contain inversion. Lines 3-4, a metaphor. Lines 4-5, a simile. Lines 5-6, synecdoche. Lines 6-7, a simile, a metaphor, zoomorphism, and a contraction, to boot. So great was Shakespeare's diction that the man could hardly drop a blot of ink without creating a trope!

What exactly is a trope? A trope is a word or a phrase that is used figuratively rather than literally. By the time students reach high school, they have normally become familiar with a few figures of speech such as metaphor, simile, and alliteration, but there are many more that they can learn which will enhance their own writing as well as their appreciation of great literature.

While learning to write, students must manage numerous aspects of language, matters like spelling, grammar, syntax, paragraph and essay form. But, in the mix, it is also helpful to provide them with opportunities to polish their writing by familiarizing them with the most poetic aspect of the writer's art—tropes, or figures of speech. The purpose of *Trope Trafficking: Figures of Speech for Classical and Christian Schools*, then, is to provide instruction in and opportunities to practice the various figures of speech that were established by the great authors of the past.

For each trope, there is a separate chapter which provides the term, its definition, and examples from various sources—literature, the Bible,[1] and great speeches, to name a few. Then exercises are provided according to the classical method: grammar stage, logic stage, and rhetoric stage. In the grammar stage exercises, students simply identify the trope in a passage that is provided. In the logic stage, students use illustrations and/or prompts to compose the trope. Finally, in the rhetoric stage exercises, students freely compose examples of the trope without the assistance of a prompt or illustration. In this way, the student moves gradually from passive recognition to active employment of the figure of speech. It is hoped that, as the ancient writers of the progymnasmata textbooks exhorted them to do, students will read their literary inventions aloud to their classmates so that all can enjoy the word play.

---

[1] In this textbook, Bible quotations are from the English Standard Version of the Bible unless otherwise noted.

Anastrophe

Pronunciation: ă-NĂS-trō-fē

Definition: Inverting natural word order for emphasis, poetic meter, etc.

Literary Examples:

Quoth the raven, "Nevermore!"

> Edgar Allan Poe, "The Raven"

Into the Valley of Death
Rode the six hundred.

> Alfred, Lord Tennyson, "Charge of the Light Brigade"

Whose woods these are, I think I know.

> Robert Frost, "Stopping by Woods on a Snowy Evening"

Linguistic Notes:

Old English, which was spoken from about AD 450 to 650, commonly employed the pattern ADVERB + VERB + SUBJECT. This sequence was natural word order and was not considered a poetic inversion.

Old English: Ða flugon þa Brytwalas to þam wuduwestenum.
Translation: *Then fled the Britons* to the fastnesses of the woods.

> *The Anglo-Saxon Chronicle*

Old English: A.D. 39 - Her onfeng Gaius rice.
Translation: A.D. 39 – *This year undertook Caius* the empire.

> *The Anglo-Saxon Chronicle*

This Old English structure (ADVERB + VERB + SUBJECT) remains today in some "frozen" expressions:

(a) Up, up, up went the balloon!
(b) There goes my reason for living.
(c) Here comes trouble!

Anastrophe Exercises

Exercise 1: Decoding

Directions: Below are some lines of English poetry which contain examples of anastrophe. Underline the anastrophe in each. (There may be more than one in each selection.)

Example:

> He clasps the crag with crooked hands;
> Close to the sun in lonely lands,
> <u>Ring'd with the azure world, he stands.</u>
> <u>The wrinkled sea beneath him crawls;</u>
> He watches from his mountain walls,
> And like a thunderbolt he falls.
>
> Alfred, Lord Tennyson, "The Eagle"

1. But when that moan had past for evermore,
    The stillness of the dead world's winter dawn
    Amazed him, and he groaned, "The King is gone."
    And therewithal came on him the weird rhyme,
    "From the great deep to the great deep he goes."

    Alfred, Lord Tennyson, *Idylls of the King*

2. Was it a vision, or a waking dream?
    Fled is that music:—Do I wake or sleep?

    John Keats, "Ode to a Nightingale"

3.   . . . thou my dearest Friend,
    My dear, dear Friend; and in thy voice I catch
    The language of my former heart, and read
    My former pleasures in the shooting lights
    Of thy wild eyes. Oh! yet a little while
    May I behold in thee what I was once,
    My dear, dear Sister! and this prayer I make,
    Knowing that Nature never did betray
    The heart that loved her.

    William Wordsworth, "Tintern Abbey"

Exercise 2: Decoding Old English

Directions: Turn these sentences from Old English works into the word order of Modern English.

Example:

>   **Source:** "The Battle of Brunanburh" (AD 937)
>
>   **Old English:** Gewiton him tha North-menn naegled-cnearrum.
>
>   **Literal Translation:** Departed then the Northmen in nailed ships.
>
>   **Standard Modern English:** *Then the Northmen departed in nailed ships.*

1. **Source:** Bede, *Ecclesiastical History of the English People* (c. AD 731)

    Old English: On þyssum ēalande cōm ūp sē Godes þēow Augustinus and his gefēran.

    Literal Translation: Onto this island came up the God's servant Augustine and his companion.

    Standard Modern English: _____

    _____

2. **Source:** "Wulf and Eadwacer" (c. AD 960)

    The speaker, Eadwacer, is worried about her sweetheart, Wulf, who has ventured out among violent men.

    Old English: Willað hy hine āþecgan gif hē on þrēat cymeð.

    Literal Translation: Will they him devour if he on force comes.

    Standard Modern English: _____

    _____

3. **Source:** "The Battle of Finnsburh" (AD 1000)

   Old English: Đā ārās mæniġ goldhladen ðeġn.

   Literal Translation: Then arose many goldladen thane. [Note: *Thane (ðeġn)* is singular.]

   Standard Modern English: _____

   _____

Exercise 3: Encoding

Directions: Use the image prompts below to compose three sentences employing anastrophe.

Volcano in Ecuador
By Frederick Edwin Church

Example: *Into the sky flew ash and flame.* _____

1.

Anastrophe: _____

_____

2.

Anastrophe: _____

_____

3.    **Anastrophe:** _____

_____

Exercise 4: Creating

Directions: Create three sentences that employ anastrophe.

1.

2.

3.

Antanaclasis

Pronunciation: ĂNT-ə-nə-CLĂS-əs

Definition: The repetition of a word in two different senses (a form of pun); the use of homonyms to create a special effect

Literary Examples:

Commenting on the dignity of the common man:

> What though on hamely fare we dine,
> Wear hoddin grey, an' a' that?
> Gie fools their silks, and knaves their wine,
> A man's a man for a' that.
>
> Robert Burns, "A Man's a Man for A' That"

Eve speaking to the Serpent in the Garden:

> Serpent, we might have spared our coming hither,
> Fruitless to me, though fruit be here to excess. . . .
>
> John Milton, *Paradise Lost*

Historical Example:

We must, indeed, all hang together, or, most assuredly, we must all hang separately.
Benjamin Franklin (1776)

Biblical Example:

Jesus then said to them, "Truly, truly, I say to you, it was not Moses who gave you the bread from heaven, but my Father gives you the true bread from heaven. For the bread of God is he who comes down from heaven and gives life to the world."

John 6: 32-34a

Antanaclasis Exercises

Name _____

Date _____

Exercise 1: Decoding

Directions: Below are excerpts from works of literature which employ antanaclasis. Underline both words in the pair and explain their diverse meanings in the space provided.

Example:

> **Antanaclasis:**
> Death, tho' I see him not, is near
> And grudges me my eightieth year.
> Now, I would give him all these last
> For one that fifty have run past.
> Ah! he <u>strikes</u> all things, all alike,
> But bargains: those he will not <u>strike</u>.
>
> Walter Savage Landor, "Age"

First Use: *To attack* _____

Second Use: *To make an agreement (strike a bargain)* _____

1. **Antanaclasis:**

   Pistol: To England will I steal, and there I'll steal.

   William Shakespeare, *Henry V*

   First Use: _____

   Second Use: _____

2. **Antanaclasis:**

   But Jesus said unto him, Follow me; and let the dead bury their dead.

   Matthew 8:22 (KJV)

   First Use: _____

   Second Use: _____

3. **Antanaclasis:**

   If you aren't fired with enthusiasm, you will be fired with enthusiasm.

   First Use: _____

   Second Use: _____

Exercise 2: Encoding

Directions: Numbered below are three unfinished statements. In each, there is an underlined two-word verb which has more than one meaning. Complete the sentence using a different meaning of the two-word verb.

Example:

One employee speaking to another:

   If these plans <u>blow up</u>, _the boss will surely blow up._ _____

1. _A detective speaking to an undercover agent:_

   We'll hook up this recorder, and then _____

   First Use:_____

   Second Use:_____

2. _At Christmastime:_

   The children's faces lit up when _____

   First Use: _____

   Second Use: _____

3. *About fundraising for charities:*

   If you want people to open up their wallets, you must first _____

   First Use: _____

   Second Use: _____

Exercise 3: Creating

Directions: Create sentences that employ antanaclasis. You may use the list of homonyms to generate some ideas, or you may use your own word pairs. You can create advertising slogans, if you like.

Example:

The squire boxed my ears for opening the forbidden box.

Homonym List

bank	cool	groom	line	tie
bat	duck	horn	order	tire
can	even	key	park	trunk
cast	fine	left	rose	wave
change	glass	lying	routed	yard

1.

2.

3.

Anthimeria

Definition: Using a word normally used as one part of speech (e.g., a noun) in the position of another part of speech (e.g., a verb).

Examples:

Phillis Wheatley
1753-1784

> **Noun used as verb:** I just *booked* a flight to New York.
> **Verb used as noun:** Phillis Wheatley *penned* a letter to George Washington.

Literary Examples:

> But ah, but O thou terrible, why wouldst thou rude on me. . .
> > Gerard Manley Hopkins, "Carrion Comfort"

> My heart in hiding
> Stirred for a bird,—the achieve of; the mastery of the thing!
> > Gerard Manley Hopkins, "The Windhover"

> The three weird sisters: Fair is foul, and foul is fair.
> > William Shakespeare, *Macbeth*

Linguistic Note:

In English, *functional shift* allows for the same word to be used in various positions in a sentence (subject, verb, object, adjective) without the addition of a suffix (e.g., nominative, accusative, genitive, etc.). It also allows a noun to be used in a verb position and vice versa. This feature of the language stimulates creative usage, as in the last statement in this set:

> **Subject:** The *school* was built in the last century.
> **Object:** We photographed the *school*.
> **Adjective:** We need to buy *school* supplies.
> **Verb:** The church *schooled* the children in the tenets of the faith.
> **Anthimeria:** *Unschool* me.

Anthimeria Exercises

Name _____

Date _____

Exercise 1: Decoding

Directions: Below are some examples of anthimeria used in advertising. Underline each example and in the space explain what language trick the advertiser used.

Example:

> **Slogan:** Nutella: "Spread the <u>happy</u>."
>
> **Explanation:** *The adjective <u>happy</u> is used as a noun (direct object).*

1. **Slogan:** Farmers Insurance: "15 Seconds of Smart"

   Explanation: _____

2. **Slogan:** Sonic: "This is how you Sonic."

   Explanation: _____

3. **Slogan:** Kroger: "Let's go Krogering."

   Explanation: _____

Exercise 2: Decoding Literary Examples

Directions: Underline and explain each example of anthimeria in the following quotations from classic works of literature.

Example:

> **Anthimeria:** I'll <u>unhair</u> thy head.
> William Shakespeare, *Antony and Cleopatra*
>
> **Explanation:** *The noun "hair" is joined with the prefix "un-" and placed in the verb position.*

1. **Anthimeria:**

> FAIRY: "And I serve the fairy queen,
>   To dew her orbs upon the green."
>   William Shakespeare, *A Midsummer Night's Dream*

Explanation: _____

2. **Anthimeria:**

> anyone lived in a pretty how town
> (with up so floating many bells down)
> spring summer autumn winter
> he sang his didn't he danced his did.
>   e. e. cummings, "anyone lived in a pretty how town"

Explanation (last line): _____

_____

3. **Anthimeria:**

> Looking in at the shop-windows of Broadway the whole
>   forenoon, flatting the flesh of my nose on the thick plate glass. . . .
>   Walt Whitman, "Song of Myself"

Explanation: _____

_____

Exercise 3: Encoding

Directions: Create a clever caption for each image below, employing anthimeria.

1. Caption: _____

    _____

    _____

2. Caption: _____

    _____

    _____

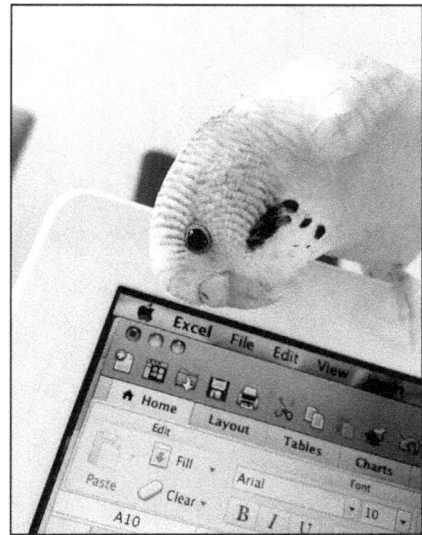

3. Caption: _____

    _____

    _____

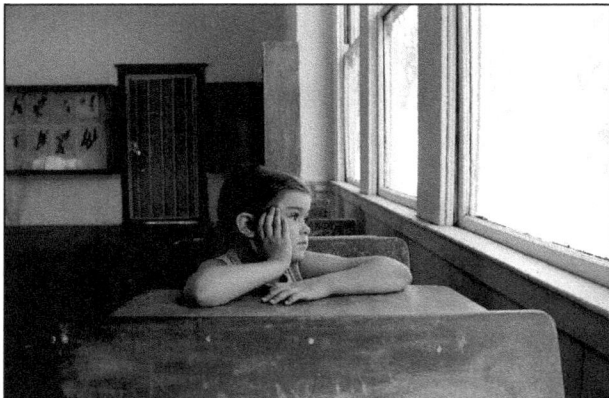

Exercise 4: Creating

Directions: Create new sentences which employ anthimeria.

1.

2.

3.

Hyperbole

Pronunciation: hī-PER-bə-lē

Definition: Exaggeration for effect

Humor:

Chuck Norris has already been to Mars; that's why there's no life there.

Chuck NorrisFacts.com

She was tougher than a grumpy she-bear and faster than a wildcat with his tail on fire and sweeter than honey, so that even hornets would let her use their nest for a Sunday-go-to-Meeting hat.

Davy Crockett, "Sally Ann Thunder Ann Whirlwind Crockett"

Well now, one winter it was so cold that all the geese flew backward and all the fish moved south and even the snow turned blue. Late at night, it got so frigid that all spoken words froze solid afore they could be heard. People had to wait until sunup to find out what folks were talking about the night before.

Paul Bunyan, *Babe the Blue Ox*

Literary Examples:

I was helpless. I did not know what in the world to do. I was quaking from head to foot, and could have hung my hat on my eyes, they stuck out so far.

Mark Twain, *Old Times on the Mississippi*

Will all great Neptune's ocean wash this blood
 Clean from my hand? No, this hand will rather
The multitudinous seas incarnadine,
Making the green one red.

William Shakespeare, *Macbeth* II.2.74-78

Hyperbole Exercises

Exercise 1: Decoding

Directions: Underline each example of hyperbole in the passages below.

Example:

> And a mouse is miracle enough to stagger <u>sextillions</u> of infidels.
>
> Walt Whitman, *Song of Myself*

1. *King Arthur, leading the Britons against the invading Saxons, with his sword Excalibur:*

   > Neither did he give over the fury of his assault until he had, with his Caliburn alone, killed four hundred and seventy men.
   >
   > Geoffrey of Monmouth, *History of the Kings of Britain*

2. *Romeo, hidden, sees Juliet on her balcony and remarks on her beauty:*

   > The brightness of her cheek would shame those stars,
   > As daylight doth a lamp; her eyes in heaven
   > Would through the airy region stream so bright
   > That birds would sing and think it were not night.
   >
   > William Shakespeare, *Romeo and Juliet*

3. They have yarns
   Of a skyscraper so tall they had to put hinges
   On the two top stories so to let the moon go by. . . .
   >
   > Carl Sandburg, "Yarns of the People" from *The People, Yes*

Exercise 2: Encoding

Directions: Use the images below as prompts to create sentences that employ hyperbole.

Example:

 **Hyperbole:** *The cold wave of 1936 lasted so long that the snowman got to march in the Fourth of July parade.*

1.  **Hyperbole:** _____

_____

_____

2. **Hyperbole:** _____

_____

_____

3.  **Hyperbole:** _____

_____

_____

Exercise 3: Creating

Directions: Compose three original sentences, employing hyperbole.

1.

2.

3.

Irony

Pronunciation: Ī-rə-nē; ĪƏR-nē

Definition: Using words to express the opposite of what is actually said

Colloquial Examples:

Your friend arrives thirty minutes late, and you say: "Glad you could make it on time today."

A child gleefully jumps up and down with excitement about a new bike, and someone says: "You can tell she really doesn't want a bike."

Literary Examples:

The usually honorable Brutus has just participated in the assassination of Julius Caesar. Caesar's friend, Mark Antony, delivers a speech in which he gradually works up to the ironic statement in the last line:

> You all did see that on the Lupercal
> I thrice presented him a kingly crown,
> Which he did thrice refuse: was this ambition?
> Yet Brutus says he was ambitious;
> And, sure, he is an honourable man.

> William Shakespeare, *Julius Caesar*

In this poem, the speaker is encouraging his friend to stop writing such melancholy poetry. Then he moves on to the friend's real problem—drink! The first two lines are ironic. The third and fourth lines reveal the speaker's actual viewpoint.

> Ale, man, ale's the stuff to drink
> For fellows whom it hurts to think:
> Look into the pewter pot
> To see the world as the world's not.

> A. E. Housman, "Terence, This Is Stupid Stuff"

Biblical Examples:

Job is exasperated with his "comforters," and says:

"No doubt you are the people, and wisdom will die with you."

Job 12:2

The prophet Elijah challenges the followers of Baal to a competition to see whose God is the true God. Baal does not respond to the prayers of his followers. We read:

And they took the bull that was given them, and they prepared it and called upon the name of Baal from morning until noon, saying, "O Baal, answer us!" But there was no voice, and no one answered. And they limped around the altar that they had made. And at noon Elijah mocked them, saying, "Cry aloud, for he is a god. Either he is musing, or he is relieving himself, or he is on a journey, or perhaps he is asleep and must be awakened."

I Kings 18:26-27

Irony Exercises

Name _____

Date _____

Exercise 1: Decoding

Directions: Below are examples of verbal irony. In the space provided, indicate what the speaker is actually saying by means of irony.

Example:

Irony: *At a theater in Mannheim, Germany:*

"In that large audience, that night, there were eight very conspicuous people. These were ladies who had their hats or bonnets on. What a blessed thing it would be if a lady could make herself conspicuous in our [American] theaters by wearing her hat."

Mark Twain, *A Tramp Abroad*

Meaning: _Wearing big hats while watching a play makes it difficult for others_

to see the stage, so Twain means this practice would not be a blessing.

1. **Irony:** *Opening line of an English novel written in 1813:*

"It is a truth universally acknowledged, that a single man in possession of a good fortune, must be in want of a wife."

Jane Austen, *Pride and Prejudice*

Meaning: _____

_____

2. **Irony:** *Socrates refers to Meletus, the young lawyer who brought him before the tribunal that would sentence him to death on the charges of atheism and corruption of the young:*

"I fancy that he must be a wise man, and seeing that I am the reverse of a wise man, he has found me out, and is going to accuse me of corrupting his young friends."

Plato, *Euthyphro*

Meaning: _____

_____

3. **Irony:** *The orphan boy Oliver Twist is brought before the orphanage board for discipline because, starving, he dared ask for more gruel:*

> "The board, in imitation of so wise and salutary an example, took counsel together on the expediency of shipping off Oliver Twist, in some small trading vessel bound to a good unhealthy port. This suggested itself as the very best thing that could possibly be done with him: the probability being, that the skipper would flog him to death, in a playful mood, some day after dinner. . . ."

Charles Dickens, Oliver Twist

Meaning: _____

_____

Exercise 2: Encoding

<u>**Directions**</u>: Use the images below as prompts to create ironic captions.

Example:

   **Caption:** *Young Adolf walks his adorable pooch, Fluffy.*

1.    **Caption:** _____

2.  **Caption:** _____

3.  **Caption:** _____

Exercise 3: Creating

Directions: Compose three original ironic statements. You may need to include a few sentences or an illustration to provide context in order for the irony to be understood.

1.

2.

3.

Litotes

Pronunciation: LĪ-tə-tēz

Definition: Understatement by using a negative to mean a positive

Biblical Examples:

"I will multiply them, and they shall not be few;
   I will make them honored, and they shall not be small."
      Meaning: They will be many, and they will be important.

Jeremiah 30:19b

Paul replied, "I am a Jew, from Tarsus in Cilicia, a citizen of no obscure city."
      Meaning: I am a citizen of a famous city.

Acts 21:39a

Literary Examples:

Zeus describing Achilles:

"He is neither unthinking, nor unseeing."
      Meaning: He is wise and perceptive.

Homer, *Iliad*

Love alters not with his brief hours and weeks,
But bears it out even to the edge of doom.
If this be error and upon me proved
I never writ, nor no man ever loved.
      Meaning: This is not error because I have written much and many men have loved.
Shakespeare, "Sonnet 116"

Colloquial Examples:

He's no Einstein.
      Meaning: He's stupid.
Not bad!
      Meaning: Good job!

Litotes Exercises

Name _____

Date _____

Exercise 1: Decoding

Directions: Read the examples of litotes, focusing on the italicized phrase, which is in the negative. Then re-write the statement in the affirmative to show the writer's point.

Example:

> **Negative:** His book was not unimportant.
>
> **Affirmative:** *His book was important.* _____

1. *Speaking of an elderly man named Victorinus:*

   Negative: He was *not ashamed* to be the child of Christ and to become an infant at your font. . . .

   Augustine of Hippo, *Confessions*

   Affirmative: _____

2. *Explaining the attitude of King Alfred the Great toward the children of his bishops, ealdormen, nobles, attendants, and friends:*

   Negative: Their sons, . . . who were bred up in the royal household, were *no less dear* to him than his own.

   Asser, *Asser's Life of Alfred*

   Affirmative: _____

3. *Referring to the lost souls being punished in Hell:*

   Negative: *Never were* persons in the world so swift
   To work their weal and escape their woe.

   Dante, *Inferno*

   Affirmative: _____

Exercise 2: Encoding

Directions: Below are statements that employ litotes. Underline the word or phrase that constitutes the liotes. Then re-write the word or phrase in its affirmative form.

Example:

> **Negative:** And [Jesus] said, "There was a man who had two sons. And the younger of them said to his father, 'Father, give me the share of property that is coming to me.' And he divided his property between them. <u>Not many days later</u>, the younger son gathered all he had and took a journey into a far country, and there he squandered his property in reckless living."
>
> Parable of the Prodigal Son, Luke 15:11-13

Affirmative: <u>*a few days later*</u>

1. **Negative:** *Describing the monster's gold hoard:*

> Within 'twas full
> Of wire-gold and jewels; a jealous warden,
> Warrior trusty, the treasures held,
> Lurked in his lair. Not light the task
> Of entrance for any of earth-born men!
>
> Anonymous, *Beowulf*

Affirmative: _____

2. **Negative:** I am not unaware that many fraudulent schemes will be found by perverted prosecutors, for which, I hope, we have devised remedies.

Claudius, "Oration on the Age of Arbiters
and on Delays in Prosecution"

Affirmative: _____

3. **Negative:** Writing a book is not unlike building a house or planning a battle or painting a picture.

Winston Churchill, "Writing a Book:
Churchill's Advice to Young Writers"

Affirmative: _____

Exercise 3: Creating

Directions: Compose three statements that employ the form of understatement that is called *litotes*. Be sure to underline the phrase that constitutes the litotes.

Example:

    Negative: *The Senate's decision to raise taxes was <u>not unexpected</u>.*

    Affirmative: <u>*expected*</u> _____

1. **Negative:** _____

_____

Affirmative: _____

2. **Negative:** _____

_____

Affirmative: _____

3. **Negative:** _____

_____

Affirmative: _____

Meiosis

Pronunciation: mī-Ō-sĭs

Definition: Understatement; the opposite of hyperbole

Literary Examples:

Romeo and Juliet? Just another chick flick.

Sherlock Holmes requests Dr. Watson's assistance in the evening:

"I shall be at Baker Street at ten."
"Very well. And, I say, Doctor, there may be some little danger, so kindly put your army revolver in your pocket."

Arthur Conan Doyle, "The Red-Headed League Is Dissolved"

Two sisters, Elinor and Marianne, are both in love, but Elinor, unlike her sister, holds her emotions in check, saying:

"I do not attempt to deny," said she, "that I think very highly of him—that I greatly esteem, that I like him."

Jane Austen, *Sense and Sensibility*

Historical Examples:

At the surrender of the Japanese days after destruction of two cities by atomic bomb:

"The war situation has developed not necessarily to Japan's advantage."

Emperor Hirohito, Surrender Speech, August 15, 1945

After losing all on-board oxygen while 200,000 miles from earth:

"Houston, we've had a problem."

Commander Jim Lovell, *Apollo XIII*, April 13, 1970

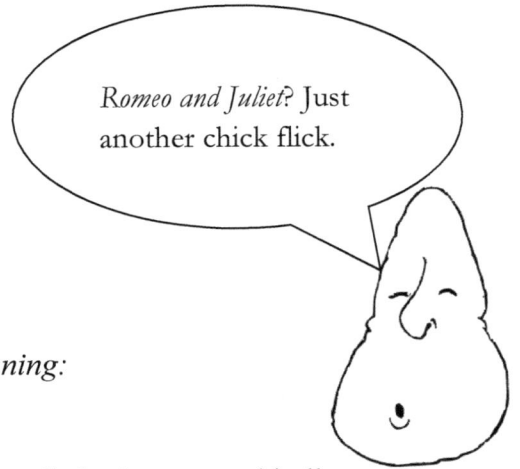

Meiosis Exercises

Name _____

Date _____

Exercise 1: Decoding

Directions: Read the following passages, each of which contains an understatement. Then, in the blank, explain what has been understated.

Example:

> **Meiosis:** Because I could not stop for Death—
> He kindly stopped for me—
> The Carriage held but just Ourselves—
> And Immortality.
>
> Emily Dickinson, "Because I Could Not Stop for Death"

> **Explanation:** *The poet understates Death's dreadfulness by saying the*
>
> *carriage held "but just Ourselves," as if it were two ordinary companions,*
>
> *and then adds "Immortality" as an afterthought.*

1. **Meiosis:**

Mercutio has been in a street brawl with Tybalt, who has run him through with a sword, causing a mortal wound:

> BENVOLIO: What, art thou hurt?
>
> MERCUTIO:
> Ay, ay, a scratch, a scratch; marry, 'tis enough.
> Where is my page? Go, villain, fetch a surgeon.
>
> William Shakespeare, *Romeo and Juliet*

Explanation: _____

_____

2. **Meiosis:**

The narrator is a poet who is bedridden with a disease. His friends try to help him pass the time by telling him stories:

> Some told of ladies, and their paramours;
> Some of brave knights, and their renowned squires;
> Some of the faeries and their strange attires;
> And some of giants hard to be believed.
>
> Edmund Spenser, "Mother Hubberd's Tale"

Explanation: _____

_____

3. **Meiosis:**

I have to have this operation. It isn't very serious. I have this tiny little tumor on the brain.

J. D. Salinger, *Catcher in the Rye*

Explanation: _____

_____

Exercise 2: Encoding

Directions: In the space provided, express the information in each statement by employing meiosis (understatement).

Example:

> **Statement:** In 2015 a woman in Wisconsin was arrested for having more than 80 living dogs and almost 70 dead dogs (mostly frozen) in her rented home.
>
> **Meiosis:** *A woman in Wisconsin was arrested for having a few extra dogs in her home.*

1. **Statement:** On June 15, 2011, an Australian-British woman named Penny Palfrey, a mother of three, became the first person to swim the 70 miles of shark-infested waters between Grand Cayman island and Little Cayman, a swim which took 40 hours and 41 minutes.

   Meiosis: _____

2. **Statement:** Barry Bonds (b. 1964), former left-fielder for the Pittsburgh Pirates and the San Francisco Giants, holds the record for career home runs (762).

   Meiosis: _____

3. **Statement:**

   > There was an old woman who lived in a shoe.
   > She had so many children, she didn't know what to do;
   > She gave them some broth without any bread;
   > Then whipped them all soundly and put them to bed.

   Meiosis: _____

Exercise 3: Creating

Directions: Compose three statements that employ meiosis (understatement) to make a statement. Then in the space provided, relate the context which explains the understatement.

Example:

   Meiosis: _My brother made a little scratch on the neighbor's car._

   Context: _My brother actually keyed the neighbor's car, and it cost $2000 to_

   have it fixed.

1. **Meiosis:** _____

   Context: _____

   _____

2. **Meiosis:** _____

   Context: _____

   _____

3. **Meiosis:** _____

   Context: _____

   _____

Metonymy

Pronunciation: mə-TŎN-ə-mē

Definition: Referring to a thing, group, place, etc., not by its own name, but by something with which it is associated. (In Greek, the word means *changed name*.)

Examples:

The president met with the *top brass*.
> [Brass is associated with the awards worn by military leaders.]

Today the *White House* announced its support for education reform.
> [The White House is associated with the President.]

Literary Examples:

This royal throne of kings, this scepter'd isle."
> [England is referenced by things associated with monarchy: throne and scepter.]
>> William Shakespeare, *Richard II*

The small deep casement sheds a ray
Which tells that in the Holy Town
It is the passing of the day—
The Vigil of Epiphany.
> [Jerusalem is called the Holy Town as it is associated with the holiness of God.]
>> Herman Melville, *Clarel*

". . . my purpose holds
To sail beyond the sunset, and the baths
Of all the western stars, until I die."
> [The west, where the sun "dies," is associated with death.]
>> Alfred, Lord Tennyson, *Ulysses*

Metonymy Exercises

Name _____

Date _____

Exercise 1: Decoding

Directions: Underline the example of metonymy in each statement or quotation below. Then explain the figure of speech.

Example:

    Metonymy: <u>The press</u> had several questions for the President.

    Explanation: <u>*"The press" actually refers to journalists, not the printing press*</u>

    <u>*equipment.*</u>

1. **Metonymy:** The pen is mightier than the sword.

                                                    Edward Bulwer-Lytton, *Richelieu; Or, the Conspiracy*

    Explanation: _____

2. **Metonymy:** I am told that this day the Parliament hath voted 2s. per annum for every chimney in England, as a constant revenue for ever to the Crown.

                                                  Samuel Pepys, *The Diary of Samuel Pepys*

    Explanation: _____

3. **Metonymy:** What has Athens to do with Jerusalem?

                                                  Tertullian, "On the Prescription of Heretics"

    Explanation: _____

Exercise 2: Encoding

Directions: Use the prompts to spark ideas about metonymy.

Example:

The decisions of the Russian leader and his advisers are sometimes called the decisions of the Kremlin, after the building where the government is housed.

Therefore, in a science fiction story set in the sea, decisions of the leaders could be said to have

come from *the Reef.* _____

1. People who went west in 1849 to search for gold in California were called '49ers.

   Therefore, people who _____

   could be called _____

2. After the Civil War, vigilante groups in southwest Missouri were called Bald Knobbers because they met on "bald knobs," grassy summits, in the area.

   Therefore, people who _____

   could be called _____

3. The world with its many sorrows is sometimes called a "vale of tears," based on Psalm 84:6, which speaks of the valley of Baka (weeping).

   Another name for the world might be _____

   because _____

Exercise 3: Creating

Directions: Create three examples of metonymy, providing an explanation for each. Then compose a sentence that shows the use of the term.

Example:

    Metonymy: _University students studying veterinary medicine could be called the "vet set."_

    Sentence: _The vet set is having a fundraiser this weekend for a new animal shelter._

1. **Metonymy:** _____

    _____

    Sentence: _____

    _____

2. **Metonymy:** _____

    _____

    Sentence: _____

    _____

3. **Metonymy:** _____

    _____

    Sentence: _____

    _____

Neologism

Pronunciation: nē-ŎL-ə-jĭzm

Definition: The creation of a new word

Literary Examples:

William Shakespeare actually created 1,700 words as he was writing his plays. This excerpt from Macbeth *shows what was—to him—a new word,* dwindle, *which we have come to know means "gradually to diminish." Here the First Witch declares what she will do to Macbeth:*

> I will drain him dry as hay:
> Sleep shall neither night nor day
> Hang upon his pent-house lid;
> He shall live a man forbid:
> Weary se'n° nights nine times nine   °seven
> Shall he *dwindle*, peak and pine:
> Though his bark° cannot be lost,   °ship
> Yet it shall be tempest-tost.

William Shakespeare, *Macbeth*

In 1931, Aldous Huxley wrote his futuristic novel Brave New World, *in which he envisioned teaching people while they are asleep by means of radio broadcast. In Chapter Two, we read:*

"The principle of sleep-teaching, or *hypnopaedia*, had been discovered."

Aldous Huxley, *Brave New World*

English-speaking novelists have often created names for characters which are not actual names in English-speaking culture. The "name" is intended to characterize the person who bore it. Charles Dickens is especially famed for these creations:

Now, *Mr. Bumble* was a fat man, and a choleric; so, instead of responding to this open-hearted salutation in a kindred spirit, he gave the little wicket a tremendous shake, and then bestowed upon it a kick which could have emanated from no leg but a beadle's.

Charles Dickens, *Oliver Twist*

Colloquial Examples:

In 1972, the word humongous *was coined by combining* huge *and* monstrous:

He had a *humongous* gash on his forehead.

In the 1990's, the word bling *or* bling-bling *was coined to refer to flashy jewelry or accessories. By 2002, it was making its way into dictionaries.*

To a baby wearing a gold necklace:

"Oh, you've got some *bling-bling* here."

Mitt Romney, Republican presidential candidate, 2008

Technology Examples:

The teacher told me to *google* more information about spiders.

The missing girl's phone last *pinged* the tower near her home at 8:47 p.m.

Have you ever crossed from England to France via the *Chunnel*?

Linguistic Notes:

In the academic community, new words are often generated by using root words from other languages, especially Latin and Greek.

- The word *psychosis* was coined in the mid-nineteenth century by combining *psyche-* (Greek for *mind*) and *–osis* (Greek for *state of disease*). It could, therefore, be expressed in English "mind disease."

- The Latin suffix *–arius* is similar to the English suffix *–er*, meaning "one who performs an action." For example, a *tabernarius* is a person who runs a shop (*taberna*). Therefore, a teacher of Latin might designate one student to be the *dictionarius*, that is, a student who would look up unknown words in the Latin dictionary and report the definition to the class.

Neologism Exercises

Name _____

Date _____

Exercise 1: Decoding

Directions: Below are some sentences containing neologisms, which appear in italic print. In the space provided, indicate what you think the word is intended to mean. EXTRA CREDIT: If the neologism involves a Latin or Greek root or a regular English suffix, include the explanation in your answer.

Example:

> **Neologism:** I feel I must inform you that my cat Snowball is actually quite *doggified*.
>
> **Meaning:** *The suffix "-ify" means "to make," so the sentence probably means that the cat has taken on the behavior of a dog, has been "made" a dog.*

1. **Neologism:** The loosening of the environmental regulations has all the *vernalists* at the *New York Times* up in arms.

   Meaning: _____

   _____

2. **Neologism:** I think my sister Maizie suffers from *Cokaphilia*.

   Meaning: _____

   _____

3. **Neologism:** Sarah's Russian spaniel was a real *cutenik* as a pup.

   Meaning: _____

   _____

Exercise 2: Encoding

Directions: Use the prompts below to invent neologisms. You may use roots or suffixes from any language with which you are familiar, but be prepared to explain your choice to the class.

Example:

> **Concept:** A female who tends to speed when she drives.
>
> **Neologism:** _speedette (adding the female suffix " -ette" to the word "speed")_

1. **Concept:** In a science-fiction story, a place where various supernatural beings are housed

   Neologism: _____

   _____

2. **Concept:** Addiction to daydreaming

   Neologism: _____

   _____

3. **Concept:** A pet name for a fast red car which suits the "fiery" personality of the driver

   Neologism: _____

   _____

Exercise 3: Creating

Directions: Create three neologisms below, providing (a) the invented word, (b) its pronunciation, if not obvious, (c) its meaning, (d) its derivation (other languages, English suffixes, etc.), and (e) a model sentence.

Example:

    a. Neologism: _cibpugarium_

    b. Pronunciation: kĭb-pəg-ÄR-ē-əm

    c. Meaning: _a cafeteria where food fights often occur_

    d. Derivation: _Latin cibbum (food) + pugna (fight) + -arium (animal pen)_

    e. Sentence: _Okay, everyone, it's 12:00. Time to head to the cibpugarium!_

1. a. **Neologism:** _____

  b. **Pronunciation:** _____

  c. **Meaning:** _____

  d. **Derivation:** _____

  e. **Sentence:** _____

2. a. **Neologism:** _____

  b. **Pronunciation:** _____

  c. **Meaning:** _____

  d. **Derivation:** _____

  e. **Sentence:** _____

3. a. **Neologism:** _____

  b. **Pronunciation:** _____

  c. **Meaning:** _____

d. **Derivation:** _____

e. **Sentence:** _____

Onomatopoeia

Pronunciation: ŏn-ə-mŏt-ə-PĒ-ə

Definition: Use of a word that makes the sound of the thing or action described

Colloquial Examples:

Splash! Pop!
Woof! Splat!

Commercial Examples:

Plop! Plop! Fizz! Fizz!
Oh, what a relief it is!

Tom Dawes, Alka Seltzer commercial, 1976

"Kellogg's Sugar Frosted Flakes! They're *Grrrrreat!*"

Tony the Tiger (Dallas McKennon), Kellogg's cereal commercial, 1951

Literary Examples (Poetry):

When all aloud the wind doth blow,
  And coughing drowns the parson's saw,
And birds sit brooding in the snow,
  And Marian's nose looks red and raw
When roasted crabs *hiss* in the bowl,
Then nightly sings the staring owl,
  Tu-who;
Tu-whit, tu-who: a merry note,
While greasy Joan doth keel the pot.

William Shakespeare, *Love's Labour Lost*

Sumer is icumen in, [Summer has come in,
Lhudé sing *cuccu.* Loudly sing, cuckoo.]

Anonymous, "Cuckoo Song"

Literary Examples (Prose):

Describing a Civil War skirmish:

Near where they stood shells were *flip-flapping* and *hooting*. Occasional bullets *buzzed* in the air and *spanged* into tree trunks.

Stephen Crane, *The Red Badge of Courage*

Describing a coach ride in France in 1845:

Crick-crack-crick-crack; crick, crick, crick; bump, jolt, crack, bump, crick-crack; round the corner, up the narrow street, down the paved hill on the other side; in the gutter; *bump, bump; jolt, jog, crick, crick, crick; crack, crack, crack. . . .*

Charles Dickens, *Pictures from Italy*

Onomatopoeia Exercises

Name _____

Date _____

Exercise 1: Decoding

Directions: Underline each word or phrase that contains an example of onomatopoeia in the passages below.

Example:

A mighty <u>banging</u> made ears valueless.

> Stephen Crane, *The Red Badge of Courage*

1.
                              and vipers crawl'd
   And twin'd themselves among the multitude,
   Hissing, but stingless—they were slain for food.

> George Gordon, Lord Byron, "Darkness"

2.   I chatter over stony ways,
      In little sharps and trebles,
      I bubble into eddying bays,
      I babble on the pebbles.

> Alfred, Lord Tennyson, "The Brook"

3. By this time my ears had grown so accustomed to the quiet, that I could hear the ticking of the clock inside as it slowly counted out the seconds. . . .

> Robert Louis Stevenson, *Kidnapped*

4. "Go a—way!" squeaked Gride, shaking his head in a sort of ecstasy of impatience.

> Charles Dickens, *Nicholas Nickleby*

Exercise 2: Encoding

Directions: Use the image prompts below to create sentences that employ onomatopoeia.

Example:

Onomatopoeia: _Dickon's arrow swished through the air and thunked into a large oak 400 yards away._

1. **Onomatopoeia:** _____

   _____

   _____

2. **Onomatopoeia:** _____ .

   _____

   _____

3. **Onomatopoeia:** _____

   _____

   _____

Exercise 3: Creating

Directions: Compose three original sentences, employing onomatopoeia.

1.

2.

3.

Paronomasia

Pronunciation: pĕ-rə-nō-MĀ-zh(ē)-ə

Definition: Creating a special effect by using two words that sound alike but have different meanings; a pun

Humor:

Q: What's black and white and [read/red] all over?
A: A newspaper.

Q: What do you call cheese that doesn't belong to you?
A: Nacho cheese.

Literary Examples (Light Verse):

Of Christopher Columbus:

But he went and tried to borrow some money from Ferdinand
But Ferdinand said America was a bird in the bush and he'd rather have a berdinand.

Ogden Nash, "Columbus"

Biblical Examples (Names):

After Phineas was killed, his wife, who was pregnant at the time, decided to name her son Ichabod, which means *inglorious*: "And she named the child Ichabod, saying, 'The glory has departed from Israel!' because the ark of God had been captured and because of her father-in-law and her husband."

1 Samuel 4:21

Jesus referred to the name of Peter, which was derived from the Greek word πέτρος (*petros*) meaning *stone*, when he said: "And I tell you, you are Peter, and on this rock (petros) I will build my church, and the gates of hell shall not prevail against it."

Matthew 16:18

Difference from Antanaclasis:

In antanaclasis, the punned word will appear in the sentence more than once:

> Put out the *light* [torch], and then put out the *light* [life of Desdemona].
>
> William Shakespeare, *Othello*

In paronomasia, the punned word will only appear once:

> Now is the winter of our discontent
> Made glorious summer by this *sun* [son] of York.
>
> William Shakespeare, *Richard III*

Paronomasia Exercises

Name _____

Date _____

Exercise 1: Decoding

Directions: Begin by looking at the examples where authors used paronomasia to create names for people or places. What point was the author trying to communicate?

Example:

>**Question:** The novel *Nicholas Nickleby* by Charles Dickens is set in an English boarding school for boys in the north of England. Intending a harsh, cruel environment, Dickens named the school *Dotheboys Hall*. What are we to understand from this name?
>
>**Answer:** *Breaking the name down into syllables reveals the name as "Do the Boys Hall." The statement "Do the boys" suggests mistreatment such as whipping.*

1. **Question:** The word *huckleberry* refers to a small, dark blue berry that grows in the wild on plants in the eastern and southeastern United States. Because they are small, the word *huckleberry* came to mean *insignificant,* and by 1835 was in use in the United States to refer to a person "of little consequence."[2] What was Mark Twain trying to say about the character Huckleberry Finn in his famous novel *The Adventures of Huckleberry Finn*?

   Answer:

2. **Question:** In the famous American short story "The Legend of Sleepy Hollow," which was published in 1820, Washington Irving portrayed the farmers and the blacksmiths as the practical men building the new nation of the United States of America. Why do you suppose he chose the name *Ichabod* for the bumbling schoolmaster?

   Answer:

3. **Question:** In ancient Greek, the word ηρα (*hera*) meant *glory*. How does that apply to the mythological hero *Heracles* (*Hercules*)?

   Answer:

---

[2] *Online Etymology Dictionary.* 2001-2005. Web. 15 July 2015. <http://www.etymonline.com>.

Exercise 2: Encoding

Directions: Create names for characters or places with the traits specified in each description below. Perhaps a Bible name would be useful, or a name based on a Latin or Greek word. Please provide an explanation for your choice as well.

Example:

> **Description:** The male character in the story cannot be trusted. He smiles in the face of his friends, but works against them behind their backs.
>
> **Name:** *Jude*
>
> **Explanation:** *The name "Jude" is a short form of "Judas," the name of the disciple who betrayed Jesus Christ for thirty pieces of silver.*

1. **Description:** The story has two brothers, one the protagonist (good guy) and one the antagonist (bad guy).

   a. Names: _____

   b. Explanation: _____

2. **Description:** A beautiful girl attracts a lot of attention but does not treat people well

   a. Name: _____

   b. Explanation: _____

3. **Description:** An imaginary land where sin does not exist and no one is ever sad

   a. Name: _____

   b. Explanation: _____

Exercise 3: Creating

Directions: Use your imagination to create two characters and one place for a work of fiction, as in Exercises 1 and 2 above. Describe the character or place, tell the name you chose, and provide an explanation for your choice.

Example:

   Description: *Setting: A lush, green place with beautiful plants and flowers.*

   Name: *Verna*

   Explanation: *The Latin word for the season of spring is ver.*

1. **Description of Place:** _____

   _____

   Name: _____

   Explanation: _____

2. **Description of Character:** _____

   _____

   Name: _____

   Explanation: _____

3. **Description of Character:** _____

   _____

   Name: _____

   Explanation: _____

Periphrasis

Pronunciation: pĕ-RIF-rə-sis

Definition: Expressing things in a way that is not clear and direct; circumlocution (sometimes employed for comic effect); called *gobbledygook* in English

Literary Example (Characterization):

A self-important naturalist speaking to Natty Bummpo about the buffalo (American bison): "I am grieved when I find a venator or hunter of your experience and observation, following the current of vulgar error. The animal you describe is in truth a species of the *bos ferus* (or *bos sylvestris*, as he has been happily called by the poets), but, though of close affinity, it is altogether distinct from the common bubulus."

James Fenimore Cooper, *The Prairie*

Textbook Prose"

"Expectancy theory focuses directly on the process of human decision making and emphasizes the cognitive processes by which alternatives are evaluated in terms of valued outcomes and the likelihood that such outcomes will occur if a given alternative is chosen."[3]

Joseph L. Massie, *Essentials of Management*

Government Gobbledygook:

"If a supplier or permissive supplier remits tax to the state, but does not receive the tax from the license holder/purchaser, the supplier or permissive supplier may take a tax a credit for the previously remitted tax on the next monthly return if the Comptroller is notified of the default within 60 days after the default occurs."[4]

State of Texas, *Motor Fuels Audit Procedures Manual*

---

[3] 3rd ed., Englewood Cliffs, NJ: Prentice-Hall, 1979.
[4] Ch. 162. 16. Aug. 2011. Web. 3 Mar. 2015.

Exercise 1: Decoding

Directions: Decode the following examples of periphrasis, which are based on popular adages, by writing the adage in the blank.

Example:

    Periphrasis: Pulchritude cannot be sustained beyond the epidermal stratum.

    Adage: _Beauty is only skin deep._

1. **Periphrasis:** Maintain stasis in equanimity.

    Adage: _____

2. **Periphrasis:** A hydrated culinary specimen under durational scrutiny will by no means effervesce.

    Adage: _____

3. **Periphrasis:** That which is attained through indolence without proper foundation will dissipate in the same imprudent manner in which it was attained in the first place.

    Adage: _____

Exercise 2: Encoding

Directions: Re-write each of these popular sayings, using periphrasis.

1. Waste not, want not.

2. "I cannot tell a lie."

3. A cat has nine lives.

Exercise 3: Creating

Directions: Create three statements employing periphrasis for comic effect.

1.

2.

3.

Prosopopoeia

Pronunciation: prō-sō-pə-PĒ-ə

Definition: Ascribing human qualities to animals or things; allowing animals or things to speak (also called *personification*)

Literary Examples:

The mournful current moved slowly on, and from the water, shaded black, some white bubble eyes looked at the men.

Stephen Crane, *The Red Badge of Courage*

The Caterpillar and Alice looked at each other for some time in silence: at last the Caterpillar took the hookah out of its mouth, and addressed her in a languid, sleepy voice.
"Who are *you*?" said the Caterpillar.

Lewis Carroll, *Alice's Adventures in Wonderland*

Biblical Examples:

Let not sin therefore reign in your mortal body, to make you obey its passions.

Romans 6:12

Wisdom cries aloud in the street,
in the markets she raises her voice.

Proverbs 1:20

Commercial Examples:

Oreo: Milk's favorite cookie!

Nabisco (Mondelēz International) Slogan, 2015

You owned your car for four years. You named it Brad. You loved Brad. And then you totaled him.

Liberty Mutual TV Commercial, 2015

Prosopopoeia Exercises

Name _____

Date _____

Exercise 1: Decoding

Directions: Read the following passages, each of which contains an understatement. Then, in the blank, explain what has been understated.

Example:

Prosopopoeia:

> . . . .so I turn once more to those who
> sneer at this my city, and I give them back the sneer
> and say to them:
> Come and show me another city with lifted head singing
> so proud to be alive and coarse and strong and cunning.
>
> Carl Sandburg, "Chicago"

Explanation: *The city of Chicago expresses the human characteristics of joy, pride, coarseness, strength, and cunning.*

1. **Prosopopoeia:**

Excerpt from a poem written upon the death of Abraham Lincoln:

> O western orb sailing the heaven,
> Now I know what you must have meant as a month since I walk'd,
> As I walk'd in silence the transparent shadowy night,
> As I saw you had something to tell as you bent to me night after night,
> As you droop'd from the sky low down as if to my side, (while the other stars all look'd on,)
> As we wander'd together the solemn night.
>
> Walt Whitman, "When Lilacs Last in the Dooryard Bloom'd"

Explanation: _____ _____

_____

2. **Prosopopoeia:**

And I looked, and behold, a pale horse! And its rider's name was Death, and Hades followed him.

Revelation 6:8a

Explanation: _____

_____

3. **Prosopopoeia:**

> I wandered lonely as a cloud
> That floats on high o'er vales and hills,
> When all at once I saw a crowd,
> A host, of golden daffodils;
> Beside the lake, beneath the trees,
> Fluttering and dancing in the breeze.

William Wordsworth, "I Wandered Lonely as a Cloud"

Explanation: _____

_____

Exercise 2: Encoding

Directions: In the space provided below each image, write a sentence or a line of dialogue that employs prosopopoeia. Focus on reflecting the mood evoked by each individual image.

Example:

Prosopopoeia: *How come all the story problems have to be in metric?*

1.

Prosopopoeia: _____

_____

2.

Prosopopoeia: _____

_____

3.

Prosopopoeia: _____

_____

Exercise 3: Creating

Directions: Compose three statements that employ prosopopoeia.

Example:

    Prosopopoeia: _The lazy raindrops slid from the eaves._ _____

1.

2.

3.

Rhetorical Question

Pronunciation: rĕ-TÔR-ĭ-kəl KWES-chən

Definition: Using a question, not to receive an answer, but to make a point

Biblical Examples:

Jesus said: "For what does it profit a man to gain the whole world and forfeit his soul?"

Mark 8:36

The Lord answered Job: "Where were you when I laid the foundation of the earth?"

Job 38:4

Literary Examples:

Say, heavenly Powers, where shall we find such love?

John Milton, *Paradise Lost*

Where are the songs of Spring? Ay, where are they?

John Keats, "Ode to Autumn"

Examples from Oratory:

"They tell us, sir, that we are weak; unable to cope with so formidable an adversary. But when shall we be stronger? Will it be the next week, or the next year? Will it be when we are totally disarmed, and when a British guard shall be stationed in every house? Shall we gather strength by irresolution and inaction? Shall we acquire the means of effectual resistance, by lying supinely on our backs, and hugging the delusive phantom of hope, until our enemies shall have bound us hand and foot?"

Patrick Henry, "Speech to the Virginia Convention," March 23, 1775

What point in the anti-slavery creed would you have me argue? On what branch of the subject do the people of this country need light? Must I undertake to prove that the slave is a man?

Frederick Douglass, "The Hypocrisy of American Slavery"

Examples of Rhetorical Question + Response:

One variation to the rhetorical question is for the author to answer the rhetorical question immediately. Look at these examples:

Who will deliver me from this body of death? Thanks be to God through Jesus Christ, our Lord!

Paul of Tarsus, Romans 7:24-25

You ask, what is our aim? I can answer in one word: victory.

Winston Churchill, Address to the House of Commons, May 13, 1940

Will no one tell me what she sings?—
Perhaps the plaintive numbers flow
For old, unhappy, far-off things,
And battles long ago.

William Wordsworth, "The Solitary Reaper"

Name _____

Date _____

Exercise 1: Decoding

Directions: Please read each example from the following lines of poetry. Then, in the space provided, explain (in statement form) what the author was trying to express in the rhetorical question.

Example:

Rhetorical Question:

> Little lamb, Who made thee?
> Dost thou know who made thee,
> Gave thee life, and bid thee feed
> By the stream and o'er the mead;
> Gave thee clothing of delight,
> Softest clothing woolly bright;
> Gave thee such a tender voice,
> Making all the vales rejoice?
>   Little lamb, Who made thee?
>   Dost thou know who made thee?

William Blake, "The Lamb"

Idea:

Blake is commenting on the providence of God for each of his creatures.

1. **Rhetorical Question:**

> Breathes there the man, with soul so dead,
> Who never to himself hath said,
>   This is my own, my native land!

Sir Walter Scott, "Breathes There the Man"

Idea:_____

2. **Rhetorical Question:**

Satan, commenting to Beelzebub about his recent expulsion from heaven:

> "What though the field be lost?
> All is not lost; the unconquerable Will,
> And study of revenge, immortal hate,
> And courage never to submit or yield:
> And what is else not to be overcome?"

John Milton, *Paradise Lost*

Idea: _____

3. **Rhetorical Question:**

After the young Scottish Lord Lochinvar rescues his sweetheart from an unwanted marriage:

> There was mounting 'mong Graemes of the Netherby clan;
> Forsters, Fenwicks, and Musgraves, they rode and they ran:
> There was racing and chasing on Cannobie Lee,
> But the lost bride of Netherby ne'er did they see.
> So daring in love, and so dauntless in war,
> Have ye e'er heard of gallant like young Lochinvar?

Sir Walter Scott, "Lochinvar"

Idea: _____

4. **Rhetorical Question:**

In Chapter One of his Civil War diary, an inexperienced Confederate soldier wrote this:

> While I was peering through the darkness, my eyes suddenly fell upon the outlines of a man. The more I looked the more I was convinced that it was a Yankee picket. I could see his hat and coat—yes, see his gun. I was sure that it was a Yankee picket. What was I to do?

Sam R. Watkins, *Co. H*

Idea: _____

Exercise 2: Decoding Rhetorical Question + Response

Directions: Each excerpt below is of the "ask-and-answer" type. Re-write each in statement form, using b*ecause*. The first one serves as an example.

1. **Rhetorical Question + Response:**

Shylock, speaking to Salarino and Solanio about Antonio, who owes him money:

> He hath disgraced me, and
> hindered me half a million; laughed at my losses,
> mocked at my gains, scorned my nation, thwarted my
> bargains, cooled my friends, heated mine
> enemies; and what's his reason? I am a Jew.

> William Shakespeare, The Merchant of Venice

    Idea: *Antonio mistreats me **because** I am a Jew.* _____

2. **Rhetorical Question + Response:**

The older Syracusan leader, Athenagoras, speaking to the younger general, Hermocrates:

> And after all, as I have often asked, what would you have, young men? Would you hold office at once? The law forbids it. . . .

> Thucydides, The History of the Peloponnesian War

    Idea: _____

3. **Rhetorical Question + Response:**

> Shall fugitives from labor be surrendered by national or by State authority? The Constitution does not expressly say. 'May' Congress prohibit slavery in the Territories? The Constitution does not expressly say. 'Must' Congress protect slavery in the Territories? The Constitution does not expressly say.

> Abraham Lincoln, Inaugural Address, 1861

    Idea: _____

4. **Rhetorical Question + Response:**

Richard, Duke of Gloucester, revealing his plot to usurp the throne of England:

> I can add colours to the chameleon,
> Change shapes with Proteus for advantages,
> And set the murderous Machiavel to school.
> Can I do this, and cannot get a crown?
> Tut, were it farther off, I'll pluck it down.

William Shakespeare, Henry VI, Part 3

Idea: _____

Exercise 3: Encoding

Directions: The statements in the exercise below are expressed in the indicative mode. Re-state each in the form of a rhetorical question.

Example:

> **Statement:** No one can stop the wind.
>
> **Rhetorical Question:** *Who can stop the wind?* _____

1. **Statement:** There is no good reason to leave this beautiful city.

   Rhetorical Question: _____

2. **Statement:** No good can come from idle hands.

   Rhetorical Question: _____

3. **Statement:** No one will ever play baseball as well as Babe Ruth did.

   Rhetorical Question: _____

Exercise 4: Creating

Directions: Compose three statements that express an opinion. Then convert each to a rhetorical question.

Example:

    Statement: _Nothing can soothe the restless soul like music can._

    Rhetorical Question: _What but music can soothe the restless soul?_

1. **Statement:** _____

    Rhetorical Question: _____

    _____

2. **Statement:** _____

    Rhetorical Question: _____

    _____

3. **Statement:** _____

    Rhetorical Question: _____

    _____

Synecdoche

Pronunciation: sĭn-ĔK-də-kē

Definition: Using a part to represent the whole

Colloquial Examples:

Could you give me a hand?

He's sticking his nose into my business.

Literary Examples:

Friends, Romans, countrymen—lend me your ears!
I come to bury Caesar, not to praise him.

William Shakespeare, *Julius Caesar*

Tiger, tiger, burning bright
In the forests of the night,
What immortal hand or eye
Could frame thy fearful symmetry?

William Blake, "The Tiger"

Biblical Examples:

Give us this day our daily bread.
Matthew 6:11

And if anyone will not receive you or listen to your words, shake off the dust from your feet when you leave that house or town.

Matthew 10:14

Difference from Metonymy:

Synecdoche refers to a part of the thing mentioned (e.g., *hand* for *body*) whereas metonymy refers to something merely associated with the thing described (e.g., *White House* for *government*).

Synecdoche Exercises

Name _____

Date _____

Exercise 1: Decoding

Directions: In the passages below, underline each word or phrase that contains an example of synecdoche. Then in the space provided explain what "whole" the part is to represent.

Example:

    Synecdoche:

        For the <u>hand</u> that rocks the cradle
          Is the <u>hand</u> that rules the world.
                William Ross Wallace, "The Hand that Rocks the Cradle"

    Explanation: *The hand of a mother on the cradle represents the way mothers*

    mold the character of the people of the future.

1. **Synecdoche:**

Jesus answered them, . . ."I give them eternal life, and they will never perish, and no one will snatch them out of my hand."

                                       John 10:28

Explanation: _____

_____

2. **Synecdoche:**

Mr. Pargetter has invited his orphan niece Nan to live with his family, though his wife resents her presence:

    MR. PARGETTER (*To his wife*): You'll 'ave Nan 'ere, and you'll stop your nagging jealous tongue.

                            John Masefield, *The Tragedy of Nan*

Explanation: _____

_____

3. **Synecdoche:**

A simple child, dear brother Jim,
That lightly draws its breath,
And feels its life in every limb,
What should it know of death?

William Wordsworth, "We Are Seven"

Explanation: _____

_____

Exercise 2: Encoding

Directions: Use the illustrations by Gustav Doré (1832-83) to practice synecdoche.   Employ adjectives to strengthen the impression you desire to create.

Example:

Choice: Choose one thing (or pair) to represent London street life in the nineteenth century.

Synecdoche: *the motherless urchin and the*

wandering goat

1.

Choice: Choose one thing (or pair) to represent medieval warfare.

Synecdoche: _____

_____

2. **Choice:** Choose one thing (or pair) to represent Old Age.

Synecdoche: _____

_____

3.

Choice: Choose one thing (or pair) to represent the sea.

Synecdoche: _____

_____

Exercise 3: Creating

Directions: Compose three original sentences, employing synecdoche. If you like, you can use the phrases you composed in Exercise 2.

Example: *The plight of the poor was evident among the motherless urchins and the wandering goats of the narrow streets.*

1.

2.

3.

Zeugma

Pronunciation: ZŪG-mə

Definition: Allowing one word (usually a verb or an adjective) to govern more than one noun in logically different applications (Greek term for "yoking together")

Literary Examples:

[They] covered themselves with dust and glory.
>Mark Twain, *The Adventures of Tom Sawyer*

She looked at objects with suspicion and a magnifying glass.
>Charles Dickens, *The Pickwick Papers*

Proverbs:

Eggs and oaths are soon broken.

Give neither counsel nor salt till you are asked for it.

Humor:

I finally told Ross, late in the summer, that I was losing weight, my grip, and possibly my mind.
>James Thurber, *The Years with Ross*

Piano, n. A parlor utensil for subduing the impenitent visitor. It is operated by depressing the keys of the machine and the spirits of the audience.
>Ambrose Bierce, *A Devil's Dictionary*

Zeugma Exercises

Name _____

Date _____

Exercise 1: Decoding

Directions: Read the following examples of zeugma. Then follow the directions to isolate the concrete (physical) and abstract meanings that are at work in the trope.

> **Example:** Underline the verb and preposition that govern the two objects of the preposition.
>
> **Zeugma:** He <u>covered</u> himself <u>with</u> dust and glory.
>
> **Concrete/Physical object of the preposition:** *dust*
>
> **Abstract object of the preposition:** *glory*

1. Underline the verb that governs the two direct objects.

   Zeugma:

   > What madness moves you, matrons, to destroy
   > The last remainders of unhappy Troy!
   > Not hostile fleets, but your own hopes, you burn.
   >
   > Virgil, *The Aeneid*

   Concrete/Physical direct object: _____

   Abstract direct object: _____

2. Underline the noun that is being described with two adjectives.

   Zeugma:

   > The ring-stemmèd vessel,
   > Bark° of the atheling, lay there at anchor,   °ship
   > Icy in glimmer and eager for sailing.
   >
   > Anonymous, *Beowulf*

   Concrete/Physical adjective: _____

   Abstract adjective: _____

3. Underline the verb that governs three direct objects.

Zeugma: "I'm Mr. Bilbo Baggins. I've lost my dwarves, my wizard, and my way."

J. R. R. Tolkein, *The Hobbit*

Concrete/Physical direct objects: _____

Abstract direct object: _____

Exercise 2: Encoding

Directions: Use the images as prompts to create statements that employ zeugma.

Example:

Zeugma: *Cleopatra stirred both hearts and poisons.* _____

1.

Zeugma: _____

_____

_____

2.

Zeugma: _____

_____

_____

3.

Zeugma: _____

_____

_____

Exercise 3: Creating

Directions: Compose statements that employ zeugma. Try experimenting with different grammatical types: verb with two objects; preposition with two objects; noun with two adjective modifiers.

Example:

First, he stole her heart and then her credit cards.

1.

2.

3.

Zoomorphism

Pronunciation: zō-ə-MŌRF-ĭz-əm

Definition: Ascribing animal characteristics to humans, things, or even spiritual beings (akin to prosopopoeia).

Literary Examples:

The fog comes
On little cat feet.

It sits looking
Over harbor and city
On silent haunches
And then, moves on.

Carl Sandburg, "Fog"

Cold, fresh wind, a black-blue, translucent, rolling sea on which the wake rose in snapping foam, and Sicily on the left. . . .

D. H. Lawrence, *Sea and Sardinia*

Biblical Examples:

If you do well, will you not be accepted? And if you do not do well, sin is crouching at the door.

Genesis 4:7a

He shall cover thee with his feathers, and under his wings shalt thou trust.

Psalm 91:4a, KJV

Linguistic Notes:

Zoomorphism can be expressed with various parts of speech:

1. **Verbs:** Use a verb normally associated with animal behavior to express the action of a human, a supernatural being, a conveyance (e.g., a train), or a feature of nature.

   Zoomorphism:

   Speaking of Man to the Ocean:

   > His steps are not upon thy paths,—thy fields
   > Are not a spoil for him,—thou dost arise
   > And *shake* him from thee. . . .
   > George Gordon, Lord Byron, "Apostrophe to the Ocean"

2. **Nouns:** Use nouns that normally refer to parts of an animal's body or to the sounds they make.

   Zoomorphism:

   A woman thought to be dead has been entombed behind the panels of a mansion which, incredibly, the woman's brother believes to be a living thing:

   > As if in the superhuman energy of his utterance there had been found the potency of a spell, the huge antique panels to which the speaker pointed threw slowly back, upon the instant, *their ponderous and ebony jaws*.
   > Edgar Allan Poe, "The Fall of the House of Usher"

3. **Adjectives:** Use adjectives that normally describe animal attributes.

   > "Catch 'im," he snapped, with a bloodshot widening of his eyes and a flash of *sharp* teeth—"catch 'im. Give 'im to us."
   > Joseph Conrad, *The Heart of Darkness*

Zoomorphism Exercises

Name _____

Date _____

Exercise 1: Decoding

Directions: Read the following passages, each of which employs zoomorphism. Then, in the blank, explain the comparison.

Example:

    Zoomorphism:

    Civil War soldier Henry Fleming fears he will lose his nerve and run in his first battle:

In the darkness he saw visions of a thousand-tongued fear that would babble at his back and cause him to flee, while others were going coolly about their country's business. He admitted that he would not be able to cope with this monster.

                               Stephen Crane, *The Red Badge of Courage*

    Explanation: *Crane uses zoomorphism to describe fear as a monster.*

1. **Zoomorphism:**

I pretended to be satisfied half-way through the microscopic meal, and the four little boys lapped up what remained.

                               Freya Stark, *The Valleys of the Assassins*

Explanation: _____

_____

2. **Zoomorphism:**

    As he is ferried across the River Styx, Virgil sees souls of the dead in the river:

        They smote each other not alone with hands,
            But with the head and with the breast and feet,
            Tearing each other piecemeal with their teeth.

                               Dante, *The Inferno*

Explanation: _____

_____

3. **Zoomorphism:**

Richard, Duke of Gloucester (later Richard III) was Shakespeare's ultimate villain. Here he describes his birth:

> The midwife wonder'd, and the women cried,
> "O Jesus bless us, he is born with teeth,"
> And so I was, which plainly signified,
> That I should snarl, and bite, and play the dog.
>
> William Shakespeare, *Henry VI, Part 3*

Explanation: _____

_____

Exercise 2: Encoding

Directions: Below are sentences in which the verb expresses an animal characteristic even though the subject is not an animal. Underline the verb in each sentence and explain the effect of the writer's use of zoomorphism in the blank provided.

Example:

Zoomorphism:

Describing Satan's rise from the burning Lake:

> Forthwith upright he <u>rears</u> from off the Pool
> His mighty Stature. . . .
>
> John Milton, *Paradise Lost*

Explanation: _Rearing up is the action of a four-legged creature, so here Milton suggests Satan's animalistic nature._

1. **Zoomorphism:**

It was unearthly, and the men were—No, they were not inhuman. Well, you know, that was the worst of it—this suspicion of their not being inhuman. It would come slowly to one. They howled and leaped, and spun, and made horrid faces; but what thrilled you was just the thought of their humanity—like yours—the thought of your remote kinship with this wild and passionate uproar.

Joseph Conrad, The Heart of Darkness

Explanation: _____

_____

2. **Zoomorphism:**

A man is being hunted like an animal. He prepares to jump into the sea to save himself:

Twenty feet below him the sea rumbled and hissed.
Richard Connell, "The Most Dangerous Game"

Explanation: _____

_____

3. **Zoomorphism:**

King Lear is shattered by his daughter Goneril's rude treatment, and, believing his daughter Regan to be more loving, says:

Yet have I left a daughter,
Who I am sure is kind and comfortable.
When she shall hear this of thee, with her nails
She'll flay thy wolvish visage.
William Shakespeare, The Tragedy of King Lear

Explanation: _____

_____

Exercise 3: Creating

Directions: Compose three statements that employ zoomorphism.

Example:

    Zoomorphism:

    Lying on the downy blanket beneath the warm sun, she was soon purring

    peacefully, lost in a dream.

1.

2.

3.

Notes

[1] Aristotle. *The Poetics*. Trans. S. H. Butcher. London: Macmillan, 1895. 22.87. *Wikimedia*. 3 Jan. 2015. Web. 8 Mar. 2016.

[2] Aristotle. 21.77.

[3] I.5.415-21.

www.ingramcontent.com/pod-product-compliance
Lightning Source LLC
LaVergne TN
LVHW081348060426

835508LV00017B/1472